HEINEMANN STATE STUDIES

Uniquely
Kentucky

Maki Becker and Michelle Aki Becker

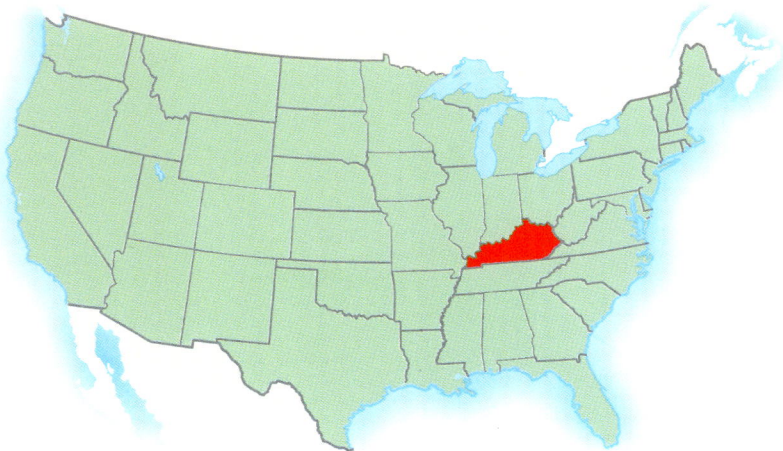

Heinemann Library
Chicago, Illinois

Designed by Heinemann Library
Printed in China by WKT Company Limited.

08 07 06 05 04
10 9 8 7 6 5 4 3 2 1

**Library of Congress
Cataloging-in-Publication Data**

Aki, Michelle, 1976–
    Uniqely Kentucky / Michelle Aki and Maki Becker.
        p. cm.—(State studies)
Includes bibliographical references and index.
Contents: Uniqely Kentucky—Kentucky's geogra-
phy and climate—Famous firsts—Kentucky state
symbols—Kentucky's history and people—The
Bluegrass Region, heart of horse country—
Kentucky's state government—Kentucky's
culture—Kentucky's food—Kentucky folklore
and legends—Sports teams—Kentucky's busi-
nesses and products—Attractions and landmarks—
Map of Kentucky.
    ISBN 1-4034-4491-9 (HC library binding)—
ISBN 1-4034-4506-0 (PB)
    1. Kentucky—Juvenile literature. [1. Kentucky.]
I. Becker, Maki, 1972. II. Title. III. Series.
    F451.3.A44 2003
    976.8—dc21

                                                    2003010352

Acknowledgments

Development and photo research by
BOOK BUILDERS LLC

The author and publishers are grateful to the
following for permission to reproduce copyright
material:

Cover photographs by (top, L-R): Corbis; Library of
Congress; Kentucky Tourism; Vince Streano/Corbis;
Bob Krist/Corbis.

Title page (L-R): Courtesy Kentucky Tourism, John
Nation, John Nation; Contents page: Photo Re-
searchers; pp. 4, 12T, 12B, 24, 27, 30, 39 Courtesy
Kentucky Tourism; pp. 6, 8, 21B, 36, John Nation;
pp. 8B, 42, 45 maps by IMA for Book Builders LLC;
p. 10 Foodfolio/Alamy; pp. 11, 17, 18, 20B, 21M,
32 Culver Pictures; p. 14T Norman Owen Tomalin/
Bruce Coleman Inc; p. 14M Ernest Schacke/
Naturbild/OKAPIA; p. 14B Anthony Mercieca/Photo
Researchers; p. 15T, Bob Krist/Corbis; p. 15M Jane
Burton/Berto/Bruce Coleman Inc; p. 15B Mark A.
Schneider/Photo Researchers; p. 16T E.R. Degginger/
Photo Researchers; p. 16B Mesza/Bruce Coleman
Inc; pp. 17, 18, 20B, 21M, 32 Culver Pictures;
p. 20 C-Span; p.21T Library of Congress; p. 22
POPPERFOTO/Alamy Images; p. 23 Andre Jenny/
Alamy Images; p 26 Courtesy LRC Public Informa-
tion; p. 29 Bruce Roberts/Photo Researchers; p. 31
B. Minton/Heinemann Library; p. 33 Walter
Sanders/Time Life Pictures/Getty Images; pp. 34,
35 Courtesy University of Kentucky; p. 37 Vince
Streano/Corbis; p. 41 Motoring Picture Library/
Alamy Images; p. 42 Reuters NewMedia Inc./
Corbis; p. 43 Courtesy Kentucky Coal Mining
Museum; p. 44 Bob Burch/Bruce Coleman Inc.

Special thanks to Renee Lynn Graves of the
University of Memphis for her expert comments in
the preparation of this book.

Every effort has been made to contact copyright
holders of any material reproduced in this book.
Any omissions will be rectified in subsequent
printings if notice is given to the publisher.

Cover Pictures

Top (left to right) Louisville slugger factory,
Abraham Lincoln, Kentucky state flag, coal miner
Main Thoroughbred horses at a horse farm

Some words are shown in bold, **like this.**
You can find out what they mean by looking
in the glossary.

Contents

Uniquely Kentucky

Kentucky is unique, a one-of-a-kind state. In 1792 Kentucky became the first state west of the Appalachian Mountains. It is home to Fort Knox, where the United States keeps $6 billion worth of gold, the largest storehouse in the world. And every year beginning in 1875, horseracing fans have gathered at Churchill Downs in Louisville to watch the Kentucky Derby, the oldest continuously run stakes race in the country.

KENTUCKY'S NAME

Many historians think Kentucky's name comes from the word *Eskippathiki,* the Iroquois name for a Shawnee town. It means meadowlands. Others say the name comes from other Native American words—"land of tomorrow" or "cane and turkey lands."

The **Cumberland Gap** *was explored and named in 1750 by Dr. Thomas Walker. Cumberland Gap National Historic Park was established in 1940.*

FRANKFORT

Frankfort is home to about 30,000 people. It became the state capital on December 5, 1792 when Kentucky became a state. It was chosen because the city promised to build a capitol, or statehouse, for the new state legislature.

Over the years Frankfort has had four different capitols. Kentuckian Gideon Shryock designed the third after the first two burned down. A limestone building with grand columns, it served as the center of government until 1910. It is the only **Union** capitol occupied by Confederate forces during the **Civil War** (1861–1865) and the only statehouse in the United States where a governor was **assassinated.** In 1900 during a heated election campaign, Governor William Goebel was shot and killed. The building is now a museum. In 1910, lawmakers moved to a fourth capitol, where legislators still meet today.

Frankfort's Name

Frankfort probably received its name in 1780 after Native Americans attacked a group of pioneers crossing the Kentucky River. One of the settlers, Stephen Frank, was killed and the crossing became known as "Frank's **Ford.**" Later the name was shortened to Frankfort.

LOUISVILLE

Louisville, the largest city in Kentucky, is located on the southern banks of the Ohio River where the river is broken up by waterfalls known as the Falls of the Ohio. During the **Revolutionary War** (1775–1783), American General George Rogers Clark built several forts in the area. In 1778 Clark and several other pioneers founded the town. They named it *Louisville* after King Louis XVI of France, in appreciation for French help during the Revolutionary War.

Louisville grew slowly. It became a city in 1828, when steamboats traveled the Ohio River. A railroad built by

*Louisville's location along the Ohio River makes it a major transportation and manufacturing center. The American Printing House for the Blind, the world's largest publisher of **Braille** products, is located there.*

James Guthrie, a Louisville business-person, connected Louisville to Nashville, Tennessee, helping turn Louisville into a trade center linking north and south.

LEXINGTON

Settled in 1775 Lexington is named after the Battle of Lexington, Massachusetts, the first battle of the Revolutionary War. Located near the center of the state, the city became a center of education soon after settlement. Transylvania University, the first in the region, was chartered there in 1780. It is also the home of Kentucky's first newspaper, the *Kentucky Gazette,* started in 1788. Today, Lexington is the second-largest city in Kentucky. It is known worldwide as a center for horse breeding.

Kentucky's Geography and Climate

Located in the east-central part of the United States, Kentucky is considered part of the South. Kentucky is bordered by numerous states, including Tennessee to the south, Illinois, Indiana, and Ohio to the north, and Virginia to the east.

KENTUCKY'S REGIONS

Kentucky's four geographic regions cover an area of 40,411 square miles. The Cumberland **Plateau,** in eastern Kentucky, has the highest elevation in the state. Black Mountain, the highest point in the state, rises 4,245 feet above sea level from the plateau. Ridges and valleys snake through the area and pine trees grow throughout the region. The Cumberland Plateau is also home to some of the state's richest coal mines.

Bluegrass Country, in northern Kentucky, gets its name from the bluish-green grass that grows across the region. The soil here contains calcium-rich limestone, which gives the grass a bluish color. The area is

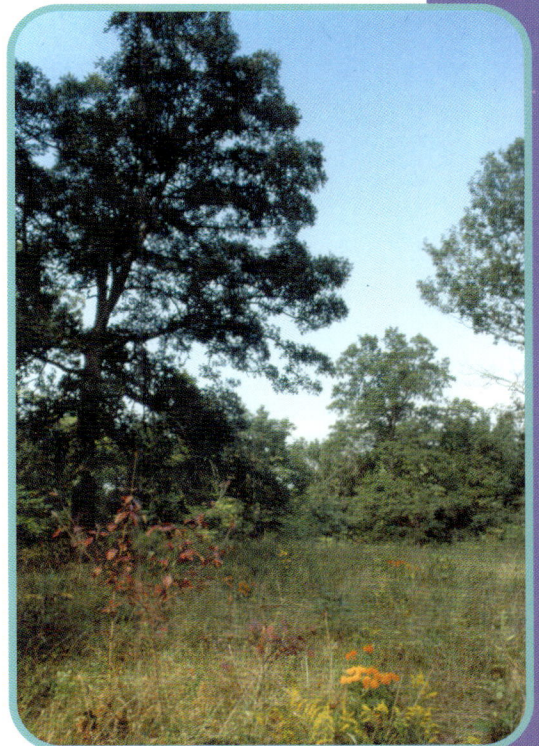

Bluegrasses have a fine-leaved foliage that is most noticeable in the month of June.

sometimes referred to as the Horse Capital of the World. Kentucky bluegrass provides nutrients that horses need, such as calcium.

In western Kentucky is a region known as the Western Coal Field. Rich coal mines dot this part of the state. The Pennyroyal, sometimes called Pennyrile, is located in southwestern Kentucky. This region is named after a type of mint that grows there. Hills and plains cover the area. There are streams underground that have carved enormous caves, each of which may be several acres in size. Mammoth Cave is perhaps the most famous cave in the area.

The region known as the Jackson Purchase lies at the southwestern tip of Kentucky. It is named for President Andrew Jackson (1829–1837). In 1818 when he was a general—before he became president—he bought the land from the Chickasaw. Jackson Purchase is surrounded by water. To the east is Kentucky Lake, to the north is the Ohio River, and to the west the Mississippi River. The area is characterized by **flood plains** with low hills. The Mississippi crosses the New Madrid Fault Line here.

Pennyroyal Mint grows wild along the roads of western Kentucky.

KENTUCKY'S CLIMATE

The word *climate* describes a region's weather over a long period of time. Kentucky has a mild, wet climate. Summers are usually warm and winters are cool. Kentucky's weather patterns are influenced by warm, wet winds that blow north from the Gulf of Mexico, especially during summer. Much of Kentucky's average 46 inches of **precipitation** a year falls in spring, the rainiest season.

Southern Kentucky receives the highest average precipitation, about 50 inches a year. The northern part of the state averages only about 40 inches.

Average Annual Precipitation Kentucky

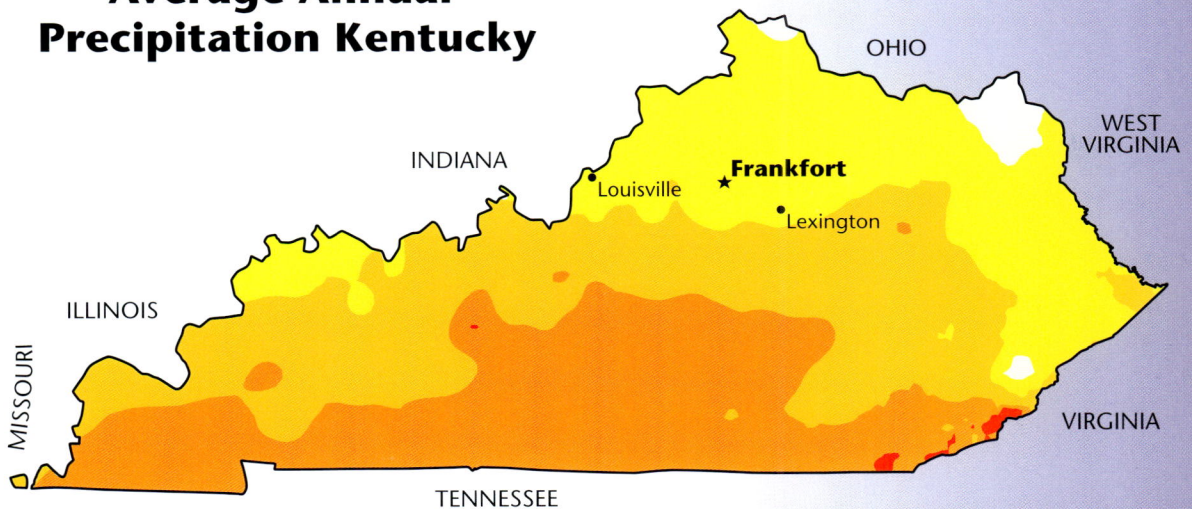

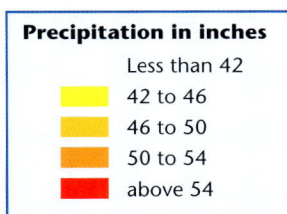

| ★ | Capital |
| • | City |

Precipitation in inches

	Less than 42
	42 to 46
	46 to 50
	50 to 54
	above 54

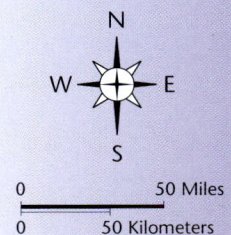

0   50 Miles
0   50 Kilometers

Famous Firsts

SOCIAL FIRSTS

In 1887 Mary Towles Sasseen, a teacher in Henderson, suggested that her pupils plan a musical program for their mothers. The event was such a success that she held a Mother's Day musical every year. Before long, Sasseen was traveling to nearby schools to help arrange similar celebrations. Sasseen died in 1906, but another teacher, Anna Jarvis, carried on the idea. She also worked to persuade others to set aside a special day to honor mothers. In 1914 President Woodrow Wilson made Mother's Day an annual event in the United States.

Louisville is the birthplace of the cheeseburger. The first cheeseburger was made at Kaelin's restaurant on Newburgh Road in 1934. According to **legend,** the restaurant owner asked his wife to put some cheese on a plain hamburger. He obviously liked the result. So do millions of people around the world who enjoy cheeseburgers in restaurants and at home.

In the United States, cheeseburgers were ranked the most popular meal for the year 2000 by a leading food magazine.

Louisville is the home of the song "Happy Birthday," which is sung at almost every birthday party in the United States. Mildred and Patty Hill, kindergarten teachers, created the song by changing the lyrics of a children's song, "Good Morning to All," to "Happy Birthday to You." The Hill sisters copyrighted the song in 1893.

INVENTIONS AND INNOVATIONS

The first time many Americans saw a light bulb was in 1883 at the Southern Exposition, a large fair, in Louisville. Inventor Thomas Edison showed off his invention to the 4,600 people who attended the fair.

People have been taking baths since ancient times. But the first enamel bathtub was made in Louisville in 1856. The tub's baked-on enamel finish made the tub safer than other tubs, more comfortable, and easier to clean. Perhaps that explains an old Kentucky law that required everyone to take one bath a year.

Edison prepared and designed his first light bulb in 1879.

POLITICAL FIRSTS

Until the 1880s citizens of the United States cast their votes in public. In 1888 Kentucky became the first state to introduce a new system of voting. In this system, voters were handed a paper ballot. They then marked their choices on the ballot in a private voting booth, where no one could watch them.

Kentucky's State Symbols

KENTUCKY STATE FLAG

The state **legislature** adopted the state flag in 1918. It features the state seal. Surrounding the seal is a circle of the Kentucky state flower, the goldenrod.

Jessie Cox, a Frankfort art teacher, designed the Kentucky state flag.

KENTUCKY STATE SEAL

The state seal of Kentucky shows two people shaking hands, representing the kindness and warmth that Kentuckians share. David Humphreys, a Lexington silversmith, designed the seal and the state legislature adopted his design in 1792.

The Kentucky seal is used on all official state documents.

State Motto: "United We Stand, Divided We Fall"

Historians believe that Kentucky's first governor Isaac Shelby chose the motto from the lyrics of "The Liberty Song" written in 1768 by John Dickinson. The song includes the words "united we stand, divided we fall."

State Nickname: Bluegrass State

Kentucky is known as the "Bluegrass State." The name goes back to the 1700s when newcomers were amazed to see the region covered by bluish grass. In fact, the grass is not really blue. It just looks blue because it has bluish-purple buds.

State Song: "My Old Kentucky Home"

Stephen Collins Foster of Pennsylvania wrote "My Old Kentucky Home" in 1853 after visiting Federal Hill, in

"My Old Kentucky Home"

The sun shines bright in the old
   Kentucky home
'Tis summer, the people are gay;
The corn top's ripe and the meadow's
   in the bloom,
While the birds make music all the day;
The young folks roll on the little
   cabin floor,
All merry, all happy, and bright,
By'n by hard times comes a-knocking
   at the door,

Then my old Kentucky home,
   good night!

Chorus
Weep no more, my lady,
Oh weep no more today!
We will sing one song for the old
   Kentucky home,
For the old Kentucky home far away.

Some people believe goldenrod causes allergies, but ragweed, which blooms at the same time, is to blame.

In May, the tulip tree blossoms across Kentucky. Its flowers look like little tulips.

what is now known as My Old Kentucky State Park. The song was adopted as Kentucky's state song in 1928.

STATE FLOWER: GOLDENROD

The goldenrod is a wildflower that blooms in the fall. In 1921, Kentucky's State Federation of Women's Clubs recommended that the state make the goldenrod the state flower because it grows across Kentucky. It also appears on the state flag. The legislature made it the state flower in 1926.

STATE TREE: TULIP TREE

The tulip tree replaced the coffee tree as the state tree in 1994. One reason for the change is that the tulip tree is the fastest growing and most adaptive tree in the state's forests.

STATE BIRD: CARDINAL

The cardinal is one of the few songbirds that stays in Kentucky during the winter. Male cardinals are bright red. Females are brown and red. The Kentucky legislature made the cardinal the state bird in 1926.

The cardinal grows to be more than eight inches in length and has a wing span of nearly a foot.

Thoroughbreds are unique because they have long necks and their eyes are far apart.

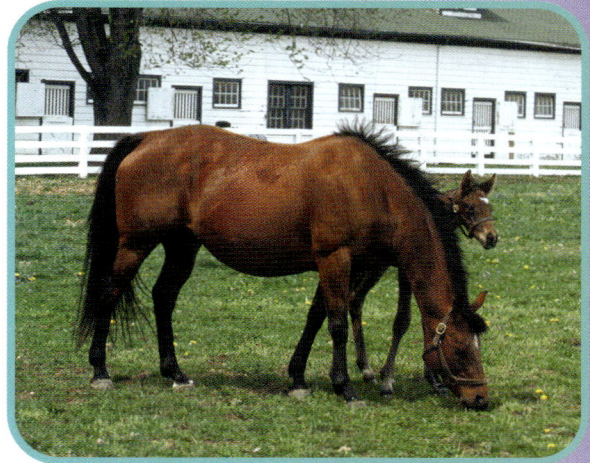

STATE HORSE: THOROUGHBRED

The Kentucky legislature selected the thoroughbred as the state horse in 1996 because it symbolizes the state's horse-breeding heritage. The thoroughbred is famous for its speed, endurance, and beauty. They are also talented jumpers and are used on hunting trips. Thoroughbreds, first bred on the Arabian Peninsula in Southwest Asia, were brought to England in the 1600s. The English first brought them to the colonies in 1730.

STATE WILD ANIMAL: GRAY SQUIRREL

As its name suggests, the gray squirrel is mostly gray with white fur on its stomach. It is about a foot long. Gray squirrels are found all over Kentucky—in rural areas and in cities and towns. The legislature made the gray squirrel the state mammal in 1968.

Gray squirrels have tails about as long as the rest of their bodies.

STATE FOSSIL: BRACHIOPOD

Different varieties of the fossil known as a brachiopod are plentiful throughout the state, which is why the state legislature made the brachiopod the state fossil in 1986.

The brachiopod, a clam-like creature, once lived on the floor of an ancient ocean that covered what is now Kentucky thousands of years ago.

Birds will not eat the viceroy butterfly·because it looks so much like the monarch butterfly.

STATE BUTTERFLY: VICEROY BUTTERFLY

The viceroy butterfly looks much like a monarch butterfly but is not poisonous. That is one reason that the Kentucky legislature chose the viceroy in 1990 as the state butterfly. The viceroy's wingspan reaches almost three inches.

STATE GEMSTONE: FRESHWATER PEARL

The freshwater pearl is Kentucky's state gemstone. The legislature chose it in 1986 because it is plentiful throughout the state. Freshwater pearls are oblong, like grains of rice, and uneven in texture.

STATE FISH: KENTUCKY BASS

Kentucky bass are found in streams and ponds throughout the state. The state legislature made the bass the state fish in 1956. It is known for its fighting ability and is considered a delicacy because it is good to eat.

Most Kentucky bass grow to between eight and fifteen inches and weigh anywhere from eight ounces to two pounds. In 1970 a Louisville man caught a seven-pound, ten-ounce bass in Nelson County.

Kentucky's History and People

The story of Kentucky goes back to prehistory—a time before anything was written down. Historians believe that six groups lived in the area between 13,000 B.C.E. and about 1650 C.E.

NATIVE AMERICANS

In the 1600s, at about the time that the first Europeans were arriving on the shores of the Americas, no Native American nation controlled the land that would eventually become Kentucky. In the mid-1600s, the Shawnee who moved into the area from places north of the Ohio River and the Cherokee and Chickasaw who moved in from places south of the Cumberland River fought for control of the region.

EUROPEAN EXPLORERS

Thomas Walker, a physician, and Christopher Gist led the first groups of Europeans through the **Cumberland Gap** into Kentucky in 1750 and 1751. The outbreak of the **French and Indian War** (1754–1763) delayed further exploration of the area until the fighting ended. In 1767 Daniel Boone, a frontier leader, visited Kentucky for

Daniel Boone (center) spent the winter of 1769–1770 in a Kentucky cave. A tree marked with his name still stands near the entrance of the cave.

the first time. Traveling with him were groups of settlers who came in search of farmland. In 1774 James Harrod, an army captain, constructed the first permanent settlement in Kentucky at Fort Harrod, the site of present-day Harrodsburg. Boonesboro was established in 1775 and other settlements quickly followed.

EARLY STATEHOOD

Virginia had claimed the land that is today Kentucky since the first Europeans settled there in 1607. By 1776 Kentucky was a county in Virginia. Soon after the **Revolutionary War** (1775–1783), many settlers urged that Kentucky become a separate state. In 1792 Congress admitted Kentucky to the Union as the fifteenth state. Isaac Shelby, a leader of the statehood movement, served as the first governor and Frankfort became the state capital.

Kentucky, a slave-holding state, had economic ties to the north and the south. But not all Kentuckians held slaves. By the 1850s, some people were **abolitionists,** while others favored slavery.

THE CIVIL WAR

After the election of Republican President Abraham Lincoln in 1860 many slave-holding Southern states seceded, or left the Union, and formed the **Confederate States of America.** Many people in these states feared that Lincoln would interfere with their right to own slaves. Therefore they decided to leave the Union and form a new nation. Some Kentuckians wanted to join the Confederacy, but President Lincoln was determined to keep the country together.

Keeping Kentucky in the Union was key to Lincoln's success. Because of its important location between the North and the South, President Lincoln once said, "I hope to have God on my side, but I must have Kentucky." At the outbreak of the war, the President sent Union troops to occupy the state and to prevent it from joining the South.

The **Civil War** (1861–1865) greatly affected all Kentuckians. Divided loyalties tore families apart, as father fought against son and brother fought against brother.

The Battle of Perryville lasted nearly eighteen hours and left over 7,000 confederate and union soldiers dead.

More than 100 battles were fought in Kentucky. The largest battle waged in Kentucky was the Battle of Perryville, fought on October 8, 1862. Confederate General Braxton Bragg hoped it would bring Kentucky into the Confederacy. But after a day of heavy fighting, he and his troops retreated to Tennessee.

The Black Patch War

Kentucky has been a leading tobacco grower since the 1700s. During the early 1900s, a group of tobacco companies tried to force the state's tobacco farmers to sell their crop at a very low price. With prices so low, tobacco farmers could not earn a living. A group of farmers in the Hopkinsville area joined together as the Planters Protective Association to fight for fair prices. Soon, violence broke out between those farmers who were willing to sell their crop for a low price and the Association. The Association began burning barns and fields of the farmers who refused to join them. Because a dark-colored tobacco was grown in the region, this fight became called the Black Patch War (1904–1909). Governor Augustus Willson sent in the army to restore peace and by 1909 the violence ended. Farmers then sold tobacco for a fair price at auctions.

Taylor was nicknamed "Old Rough and Ready" because of his military background.

After the fall of the Confederacy in 1865 Jefferson Davis was imprisoned until 1867.

During the war, about 30,000 soldiers from Kentucky died from battle wounds, accidents, and disease. Although some Louisville businesses prospered, many farmers lost crops and livestock to both armies. After almost four years of fighting, the Confederacy surrendered in April 1865, and the Union was saved.

FAMOUS PEOPLE

Zachary Taylor (1784–1850), U.S. President. Although Taylor was born in Virginia in 1784 his family moved to Kentucky when he was a baby. Taylor joined the army and eventually became a general. He became famous during the War with Mexico (1846–1848). He was elected the twelfth president of the United States in 1848 but served only sixteen months before he became sick and died on July 9, 1850.

Jefferson Davis (1808–1889), politician. Davis was born in Fairview, Kentucky. He graduated from West Point Military Academy, served in the U.S. army, and then became a cotton planter in Mississippi. He served in the U.S. Senate from 1847 to 1851 and then again from 1857 to 1861. He also served as the U.S. secretary of war from 1853 to 1857. A strong defender of **states' rights,** Davis favored **secession** from the United States. He served as the only president of the Confederate States of America (1861–1865).

Abraham Lincoln (1809–1865), U.S. President. Abraham Lincoln was born in Hodgenville, Kentucky, where he lived until he was seven years old. Elected to the

presidency in 1860, he led the Union against the Confederacy during the Civil War. Lincoln believed that the Union could not be broken. During the war, Lincoln issued the Emancipation Proclamation, freeing the slaves in the Confederacy. On April 14, 1865, near the end of the war, John Wilkes Booth shot Lincoln at Ford's Theater in Washington, D.C. He died the next day.

Carry A. Nation (1846–1911), reformer. Born in Gerrard County, Carry Nation was one of the first women **reformers** in the United States. A devout Christian, she helped organize the Women's Christian Temperance Union, a group that campaigned against the evils of drinking alcohol. She is often remembered for her use of a hatchet to destroy saloons.

Bill Monroe (1911–1996), musician. William Smith Monroe is considered the father of bluegrass music. Bluegrass is played by a band usually made up of a guitar, a five-string banjo, a mandolin, a fiddle, and a string bass. Monroe was born near Rosine. His uncle taught him to play the guitar, fiddle, and the mandolin.

Carry Nation received gifts of hatchets from her supporters across the country.

Bill Monroe and his band, the Bluegrass Boys, became famous in the 1940s.

He wrote Kentucky's official bluegrass song, "Blue Moon of Kentucky."

Muhammad Ali (1942–   ), boxing champion. Born Cassius Clay in Louisville, Ali started boxing at the age of twelve after someone stole his bicycle. After winning the gold medal at the 1960 summer Olympics in Rome, he turned professional. In 1964 Clay announced that he had converted to **Islam** and changed his name to Muhammad Ali. He eventually set a lifetime record of 56 wins in the ring. Ali is considered the greatest fighter of all time and is one of the world's most famous athletes. Since retiring from boxing, Ali has traveled the world promoting peace and racial tolerance. He lit the Olympic flame at the 1996 Olympics in Atlanta.

Muhammad Ali, diagnosed with Parkinson's disease in 1982, set up the Ali Center to help care for people with the illness.

The Bluegrass Region— Heart of Horse Country

Kentucky is famous for its champion horses and the Kentucky Derby, an annual horserace watched by millions of fans. Raising horses has been a part of life in Kentucky since the 1700s when people raced their horses through the streets of Louisville.

Kentuckians breed and raise horses for show and racing. The horseracing industry is important to the state's economy. It makes about $20 million in **tax revenues** for the state every year.

THE THOROUGHBRED

The Thoroughbred is a special horse, with long sloping shoulders and a graceful neck. Their thin legs and long hind legs help the horses reach speeds of up to 40 miles per hour. Its speed makes the muscular and powerful thoroughbred an excellent racing horse.

About 450 horse farms dot the Bluegrass Region—with about 150 in the Lexington/Fayette County area alone.

The track at Churchill Downs is a famous mile and a quarter long.

The Thoroughbred is bred from three different kinds of horses—the Darley Arabian, Godolphin Arabian, and Byerly Turk. The best Thoroughbreds may sell for more than $10 million each!

CHURCHILL DOWNS—THE KENTUCKY DERBY

Churchill Downs is the home of the Kentucky Derby. Meriwether Lewis Clark Jr., the grandson of William Clark who, together with Meriwether Lewis, explored the Louisiana Territory in 1804 and 1805, built the track in the early 1870s in Louisville.

The first Kentucky Derby Race took place on May 17, 1875. The race did not gain much national attention until 1902, when Colonel Matt J. Winn, a horseracing enthusiast, bought the track and began promoting the race. By 1920, the Derby was the best known horserace in the United States.

Today, the Derby takes place on the first Saturday in May. Thousands of people from around the world come to Kentucky to watch the race along with the millions who watch the race on television.

The Kentucky Derby is the first of three races, which together are called the **Triple Crown.** The second, the Preakness Stakes, is held in Baltimore, Maryland, on the third Saturday of May. The third race, the Belmont Stakes, is held in Elmont, New York, on the second Saturday of June.

Derby Festivities

The actual Kentucky Derby lasts only about two minutes. Nevertheless, Louisville has made a tradition of throwing a two-week party to celebrate. The occasion is marked by more than 70 events, including parades, dances, fireworks displays, hot-air balloon races, cook-offs, and a spelling bee.

Kentucky's State Government

Kentucky's government is based in Frankfort, the capital. The state is governed by a **constitution.** The constitution that governs Kentucky today went into effect in 1891. It promises many freedoms for Kentucky's people, including freedom of religion, speech, and the press. These basic rights are based on those listed in the U.S. Constitution. Like the **federal government** in Washington,

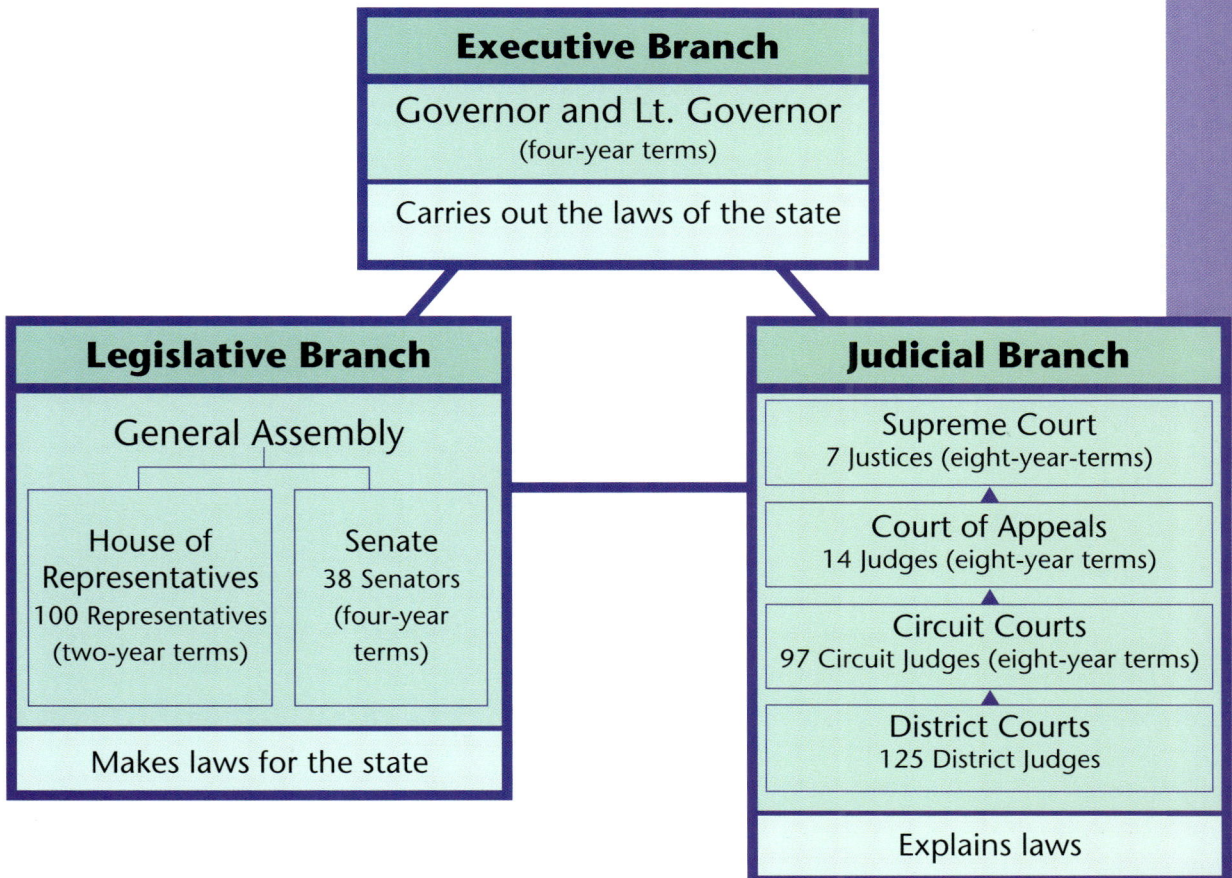

Executive Branch

Governor and Lt. Governor
(four-year terms)

Carries out the laws of the state

Legislative Branch

General Assembly

House of Representatives	Senate
100 Representatives (two-year terms)	38 Senators (four-year terms)

Makes laws for the state

Judicial Branch

Supreme Court
7 Justices (eight-year-terms)

▲

Court of Appeals
14 Judges (eight-year terms)

▲

Circuit Courts
97 Circuit Judges (eight-year terms)

▲

District Courts
125 District Judges

Explains laws

The Kentucky legislature meets in a chamber on the third floor of the capitol building.

D.C., Kentucky's government is made up of three branches—the legislative, executive, and judicial.

THE LEGISLATIVE BRANCH

Kentucky's **legislature,** called the General Assembly, makes the state's laws. It consists of two houses—the senate and the house of representatives. The senate's 38 members are elected to 4-year terms. The house's 100 members are elected to 2-year terms. Kentucky's legislators are not restricted by term limits.

A bill, or proposed law, may start in either house of the General Assembly, except for bills about taxes. These bills must start in the house of representatives. When a bill has been approved by a majority, or more than half, of the members of both houses, it is sent to the governor. If the governor signs the bill, it becomes a law. If the governor vetoes, or rejects, the bill, it becomes law only if a majority of the legislature votes to override the veto.

THE EXECUTIVE BRANCH

The executive branch enforces the state's laws and runs the state from day to day. The governor is the head of this branch. The lieutenant governor is the second-highest state official. Voters elect these two government leaders to a four-year term of office. The governor is limited to two four-year terms.

Voters also elect other officials in the executive branch, such as the secretary of state, to four-year terms. The secretary of state helps new businesses get started by registering them, and he or she also registers voters.

THE JUDICIAL BRANCH

The judicial branch decides how the state's laws apply to particular cases. The courts in Kentucky include district courts, circuit courts, a court of appeals, and a Supreme Court.

District courts have limited **jurisdiction.** They hear cases involving children and teenagers, **misdemeanors,** traffic offenses, and **civil cases** involving $4,000 or less. Ninety percent of all Kentuckians involved in court dealings appear in district court.

The circuit courts hear cases involving more than $4,000. Circuit courts have jurisdiction over cases involving **capital offenses, felonies,** divorces, adoptions, and land disputes.

The court of appeals reviews cases that have been heard in a district or circuit court. If the losing parties are not satisfied with a ruling, they may ask the court of appeals to review the decision.

Massive marble stairways on the outside of the capital building were modeled after the Paris Grand Opera House. They lead to the second floor, or judicial floor, where Kentucky's Supreme Court is located.

The Kentucky Supreme Court is the most powerful court in the state. It hears cases that have not been settled in other state courts. Cases which involve the death penalty, life imprisonment, or imprisonment for twenty years or more go directly from the circuit court where the cases were tried, to the Supreme Court for review. Seven justices from seven appellate districts are elected to the Supreme Court for eight-year terms. The chief justice is chosen for a four-year term by the other justices.

Kentucky's Culture

Kentucky's culture is diverse. The state's people celebrate their heritage with shows, festivals, and contests.

THE AURORA COUNTRY FESTIVAL

The annual Aurora Country Festival is held every October near Kentucky Lake in the southwestern part of the state. The three-day festival celebrates the state's country heritage. It features craft demonstrations such as broom tying, quilt making, and sorghum making. Sorghum syrup is made from sugar cane and is used as a sweetener. Homemade specialties—jams, jellies, pies, and cakes—are featured at the festival. Lumberjacks demonstrate their skill in events such as the ax throw, the two-person cross-cut, and the underhand log chop.

The festival features entertainment, including bluegrass bands and square dancing. Visitors enjoy Kentucky favorites such as fried chicken, barbeque, and corn on the cob.

The Kentucky Quilt Project

The Kentucky Quilt Project was one of the first organizations started to promote an interest in the craft of quilting. It was founded in 1981 by Eleanor Bingham Miller, Eunice Sears, Dorothy West, and Shelly Zegart in Lexington. The group started a yearly practice of having "Quilt Days" which were held with the goal of finding fine and unique examples of antique quilts. Today, there are "Quilt Days" held all over the country.

APPALACHIA AND RURAL LIFE

The Appalachian region in eastern Kentucky is rural and offers a traditional way of life. Because of the rugged landforms of this region, the original Scotch-Irish settlers of the area were cut off from the rest of the state until recently. Their isolation helped them preserve traditional crafts such as quilting, doll making, and basket making.

In the Appalachian region, some people use expressions that date back to colonial times. Unique language patterns are found in the region. For example, "He acted right ill with me" means that the person was angry and had poor manners. "I got some ginnin' to do" means that there are chores and errands to run.

Music has always been an important part of Appalachian culture. The music reflects the musical traditions of European colonists as well as those of people of African descent. Many Appalachian songs are ballads, songs that tell a story. Some examples of ballads are "Barbara Allen," "Old Joe Clark," and "Mister Frog Went A-Courtin." Fiddles, banjos, and the dulcimer, a musical instrument brought to the Americas by settlers in the 1700s, are used to play many Appalachian ballads.

The dulcimer was first played in the Middle East, and brought to Europe over 800 years ago. European explorers introduced the instrument to the Appalachian region in the 1700s.

Kentucky's Food

Kentucky's food reflects its southern heritage. From deep fried treats and grits to rich desserts, the dishes associated with Kentucky are the kinds of foods found throughout the south.

DERBY PIE

Derby pie is a lip-smacking dessert served at parties and restaurants across Kentucky. It is made with chocolate chips and nuts, either walnuts or pecans—and has been a favorite in the region since the mid-1900s. It was probably first served at the Melrose Inn in Prospect, Kentucky, by George Kern, the restaurant manager. The pie was so popular that Kern **patented** his recipe in 1968.

Colonel Sanders

Harland Sanders was born in 1890. He developed his special recipe back in the 1930s when he operated a roadside restaurant and motel in Corbin, Kentucky. His blend of eleven herbs and spices developed a loyal following at the Sanders Court & Cafe. In 1935 Kentucky's governor, Ruby Laffoon, tried Sanders' chicken and liked it so much he made him an honorary colonel. KFC Corporation, based in Louisville, is the world's largest chicken restaurant chain with stores in more than 80 countries.

Recipe for Kentucky Chocolate Pecan Pie

Be sure to have an adult help you with this recipe.

2 eggs, beaten

½ cup butter or margarine, melted

¼ cup cornstarch

1 cup sugar

1 cup of whole pecans or walnuts

1 12 oz. bag of chocolate chips

1 9-inch ready-made pie crust—unbaked

Pre-heat oven to 350° F. In a large bowl, mix all of the ingredients. Carefully pour into the pie shell. Bake the pie in the oven for about 45 minutes. Let cool about half an hour; serve warm with a big helping of whipped cream.

DERBY GRITS WITH RED-EYE GRAVY

A genuinely Southern dish is grits with gravy. Grits are made from cornmeal mixed into boiling water or milk. The result is a thick, hearty breakfast dish. Some people add butter or cheese to enhance the flavor. Many Southerners pour red-eye gravy over their serving of grits. Red-eye gravy combines two very different ingredients—fat drippings from country ham, which is a salty pork product, and strong coffee.

Kentucky's Folklore and Legends

Legends and folklore are stories that are not totally true, but are often based on bits of truth. These stories help people understand things that cannot be easily explained. They also teach lessons to younger generations. People from Kentucky have told many such stories through the years.

CASEY JONES

John Luther Jones was born in Cayce, Kentucky, in 1863. He was called "Casey" after his hometown of Cayce. Jones loved trains and worked for Illinois Central Railroad as an engineer.

Although Jones was known for bringing his trains in on time, he took risks. On April 29, 1900, a fellow worker

Casey Jones became an American folk hero after Wallace Saunders, an African American railroad worker, wrote a song about the tragic accident.

called in sick and Jones took his shift. The scheduling change led to a delay of more than an hour, and Jones decided to make up the time. Suddenly, Jones saw a train stopped on the tracks. He pulled on the brakes, but it was too late. His train could not stop in time and crashed into the **caboose** of the other train. Jones was killed in the crash.

THE HATFIELDS AND THE MCCOYS

The Hatfields and the McCoys lived near the border between Kentucky and West Virginia. The **feud** between the two families started in 1878. The Hatfields and the McCoys both owned land in **rural** Tug Valley, Kentucky. The two farm families lived peacefully until the day in 1878 that Randolph McCoy accused Floyd Hatfield of stealing a pig. They took the fight to court, setting the stage for more than a century of rivalry.

Despite a court's decision in favor of Floyd Hatfield, the feud continued and sometimes turned violent. As the years passed, Tug Valley became famous for its timber. As demand for wood grew, the Hatfields and the McCoys began fighting over land rights. The fight eventually turned into a feud between Kentucky and West Virginia.

The McCoys lived on the Kentucky side of the Tug River, and the Hatfields lived on the West Virginia side.

Kentucky's Sports Teams

Although Kentucky is not home to any major professional sports teams, Kentuckians are proud of their college and high school teams. Kentucky is also home to two minor league baseball teams, the Louisville Bats and the Lexington Legends.

THE WILDCATS

The University of Kentucky (UK) offers many school sports, including basketball, volleyball, soccer, and football teams. However, UK is famous for basketball.

The UK Wildcats have won seven men's basketball national championships, many of them under head coach Adolph Rupp. Rupp began coaching the Wildcats in 1930 and continued for 42 years. One of the winningest coaches of all time, Rupp's lifetime record at UK is 876 wins and only 190 losses.

The Wildcats play in Rupp Arena. It is named in honor of Adolph Rupp who led the team to its first national championship in 1948.

The UK Wildcats

According to legend, the nickname "Wildcats" started after the university's football team beat the University of Illinois in the fall of 1909. After that game, Commandant Phillip Carbusier, who was in charge of the military department at UK, is said to have declared that the Kentucky team "fought like wildcats." The name stuck and now the university's teams are called the Wildcats.

UK basketball pride is on display at the unique University of Kentucky Basketball Museum. Visitors to the museum can play a virtual one-on-one with Wildcat legends, and call play-by-play for a favorite game.

MINOR LEAGUE BASEBALL

Kentucky hosts the Louisville Bats, the AAA team for the Cincinnati Reds. Until 1999 when the team was associated with the St. Louis Cardinals, they were called the Redbirds. In 2003 the Louisville Bats were the International League Western Division Champions. However, the Bats narrowly lost to the Durham Bulls in the league's playoffs.

The Lexington Legends, an A-class team for the Houston Astros, began playing in 2001. In their first year of existence, Lexington won the South Atlantic League Championship. In 2003 Lexington finished second in their division but lost in the semi-finals of the league's playoffs.

Kentucky's Businesses and Products

Kentucky has a variety of farms, factories, and other industries that fuel its economy. These businesses rely on local resources and the skills of Kentucky's workers.

FARM PRODUCTS

Kentucky farmers grow tobacco, corn, and soybeans and raise horses and cattle on the states almost 100,000 farms. Tobacco is Kentucky's number one **cash crop.** It is the second largest producer of tobacco in the country. In corn and soybean production, Kentucky ranks fourteenth among the states. Kentucky's agriculture is valued at more than three billion dollars a year.

In the year 2000, there were 91,000 farms in Kentucky covering over eleven million acres.

In 2000 Kentucky coal miners made an average of $43,000 per year.

INDUSTRY

Manufacturing is extremely important to Kentucky's economy. More than $30 billion of the state's revenue comes from such diverse manufacturing industries, as clothing, electronics, industrial machinery, and transportation equipment.

MINING

Kentucky is the third-largest producer of coal in the United States. It first became a major industry in the 1870s and reached its peak in the early 1900s.

Two coalfields produce most of the state's coal today. One is located in a part of the Appalachian Basin Coal Field in eastern Kentucky and the other is in the Interior Basin Coal Field in western Kentucky. Together, these coalfields account for nearly 85 percent of the state's total mining. More than 150 million tons are produced annually throughout the state. The coal industry employs more than 70,000 Kentuckians.

In recent years, Kentucky's coal mining companies have begun one of the most environmentally significant tasks in the nation—the reclamation of mined lands. Reclamation means returning the land to its original condition or to another productive use. Most of the reclaimed land is invisible. Unless there is a sign nearby, it is hard to tell that a site was once an active coalmine.

TOURISM

Tourism in Kentucky creates about 144,000 jobs statewide. In addition, the tourism and travel industry adds more than seven billion dollars to Kentucky's economy and $783 million in local and state tax moneys. Kentuckians' hospitality is legendary, from the urban area of Louisville to the smaller cities and towns that date back to the original travels of Daniel Boone.

Fort Knox

The U.S. government established Fort Knox, located in Hardin County, during **World War I** (1914–1918) to train the military. During **World War II** (1941–1945), it became the secret hiding place of important historical documents, including the original copies of the U.S. Constitution and the **Bill of Rights.** These documents were hidden to keep them safe. Today, the fort is used to store about six billion dollars worth of the country's gold. The gold, kept in a heavily guarded underground vault, is the largest amount of gold stored anywhere in the world.

Attractions and Landmarks

Kentucky is known for the natural beauty of its land and the historical importance of its landmarks. Every year, people from all over the world travel to the state to enjoy its many attractions.

HISTORIC SITES

The sixteenth president of the United States, Abraham Lincoln, was born in Hodgenville, Kentucky, on February 12, 1809. His parents were farmers who lived in a log cabin on a farm there. Today the farm is known as the Abraham Lincoln Birthplace National Historic Site and Boyhood Home.

A huge marble monument covers the Lincoln's **reconstructed** log cabin. Visitors climb 56 steps to reach the building—a step for each year of Lincoln's life. Carved into the building's doorway are the words, "Here over the log cabin where Abraham Lincoln was born, destined to preserve the Union and free the slave, a grateful people have dedicated this memorial to unity, peace, and brotherhood among the states." People can learn more

The Lincoln Birthplace Monument was completed in 1911.

Places to See in Kentucky

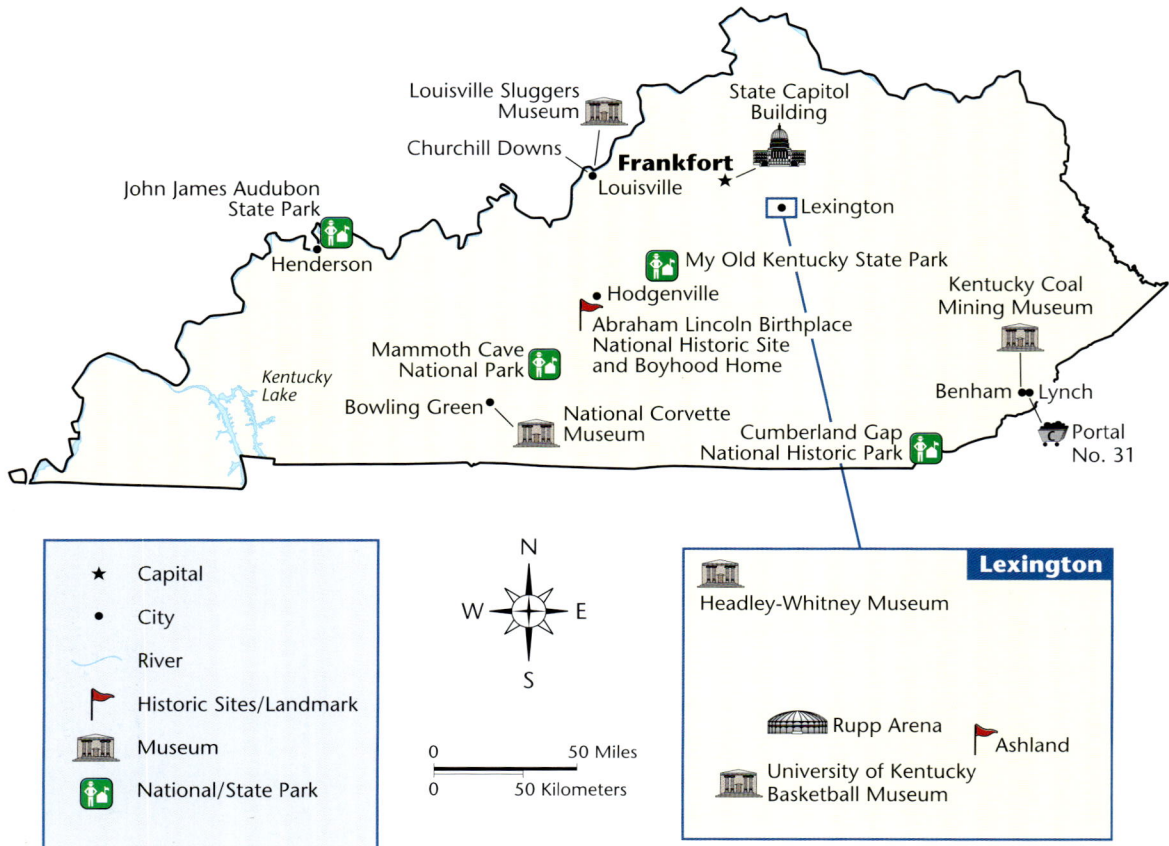

Map legend:
- ★ Capital
- • City
- River
- ⚑ Historic Sites/Landmark
- 🏛 Museum
- 🏞 National/State Park

Scale:
0 — 50 Miles
0 — 50 Kilometers

Map labels:
- Louisville Sluggers Museum
- Churchill Downs
- **Frankfort**
- Louisville
- State Capitol Building
- Lexington
- John James Audubon State Park
- Henderson
- My Old Kentucky State Park
- Hodgenville
- Abraham Lincoln Birthplace National Historic Site and Boyhood Home
- Kentucky Coal Mining Museum
- Mammoth Cave National Park
- Benham • Lynch
- Kentucky Lake
- Bowling Green
- National Corvette Museum
- Cumberland Gap National Historic Park
- Portal No. 31

Lexington inset:
- Headley-Whitney Museum
- Rupp Arena
- Ashland
- University of Kentucky Basketball Museum

about the site and the life of Abraham Lincoln at the visitor center.

Many visitors to Lexington tour Ashland, the estate built by Henry Clay. Clay served as a Kentucky state legislator, a U.S. Senator (1806–1807; 1810–1811; 1831–1842; 1849–1852), and Speaker of the House of Representatives. He is known as "The Great Compromiser" because he put together the **Missouri Compromise of 1820** and the **Compromise of 1850.**

Clay's estate is a two-story brick mansion. Following his death in 1852, the house was in poor condition. In 1857, Clay's son rebuilt the home on its first foundation, copying the original design. In the 1990s many of the Clay family's belongings were returned to the home. The first floor of the mansion shows the rooms as they looked in the 1880s. Henry Clay's bedroom on the second floor displays important items from his life and political career. Twenty acres of the original estate remain, including the gardens. Ashland was made a National Historic Landmark in 1960 and is open to visitors.

UNIQUE MUSEUMS

Every Corvette, a Chevrolet sports car, is produced in Bowling Green, at the General Motors Assembly Plant there. At the nearby National Corvette Museum, visitors can learn about the history of this sleek and powerful automobile. For example, in 1953 the first year of production, only 300 Corvettes were made—all were white with a red interior. Ten years later, the plant turned out

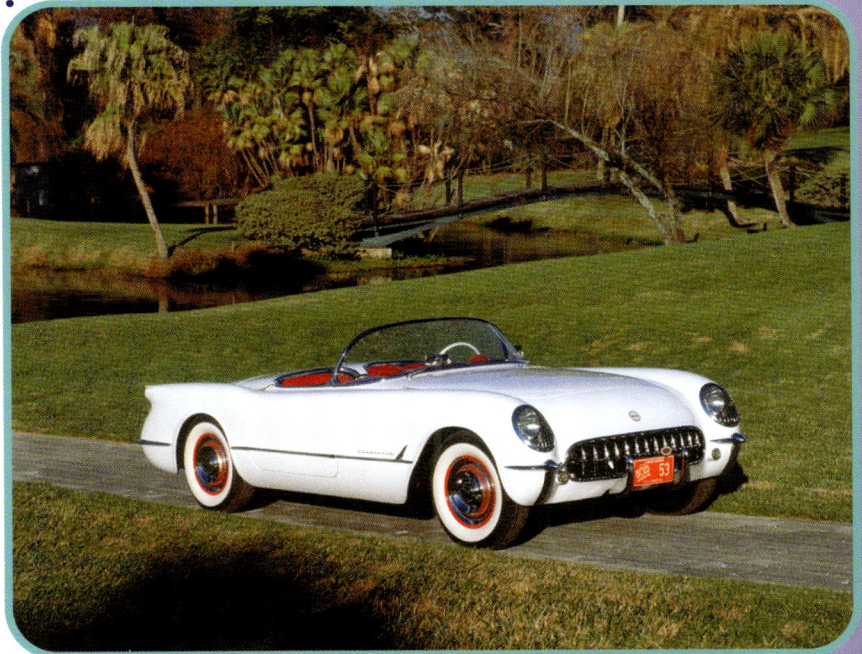

The first Covettes began being made on June 30, 1953 in Flint, Michigan. By the end of the year the three hundred cars had been created entirely by hand, and sold to the public for $3,498.

Louisville Sluggers have been crafted locally since 1884.

more than 21,000 Corvettes. By 2002 the assembly plant turned out more than 35,000 automobiles. Visitors can also walk across the street and tour the assembly plant to see how Corvettes are made.

The Louisville Sluggers Museum honors perhaps the most famous baseball bat in the world. It is home to the world's largest bat, which is 120-feet long and weighs 68,000 pounds. Louisville Sluggers used by Ty Cobb and Lou Gehrig are displayed. The autographed bat Hank Aaron used when he hit his 700th homerun is also there. Some hitters know exactly how their bats are supposed to feel. Ted Williams once returned a batch of bats, complaining that they did not feel right. The factory remeasured the grips and discovered that the circumference was off by .005 inches!

Located in Lexington, the Headley-Whitney Museum is made up of three buildings located on the family farm of George W. Headley III (1908–1985). He was a jewelry designer who collected decorative crafts from around the world. Originally from Kentucky, Headley studied art in New York and in Paris. He then started a successful jewelry business in California that was popular among movie stars. Today, the museum is dedicated to Headley's extensive collection of decorative art. The works on display include vases, ceramics, furniture, clothing, and textiles.

The Kentucky Coal Mining Museum opened its doors to the public for the first time in May 1994.

The Kentucky Coal Mining Museum, located in Benham, offers visitors insight into the daily lives of coalminers. Four stories house 30 exhibits that show examples of their working conditions, homes, and the **company store.** In nearby Lynch, visitors can tour Portal No. 31, Kentucky's first coal mine. First opened in 1917, Portal No. 31 was the world's largest coal camp at the time. In 1923 the mine set a world record for producing the most coal—12,820 tons—in a nine-hour shift. The coal filled 256 railroad cars.

KENTUCKY PARKS

John James Audubon, who is famous for studying and drawing birds in the wild, spent several years in the woods of Henderson, Kentucky, studying the area's unique birds. In the early 1800s Audubon drew hundreds of pictures of birds and tried to get a book of his illustrations published. No one in the United States was interested, so he took the book to England where it was published in 1826 and widely praised.

Today, there is a wildlife observatory and a museum of Audubon's life-size, realistic drawings. Visitors can also stay overnight at a camp or cottage in the state park. Fishing, hiking, and bird watching are some of the activities featured at the park.

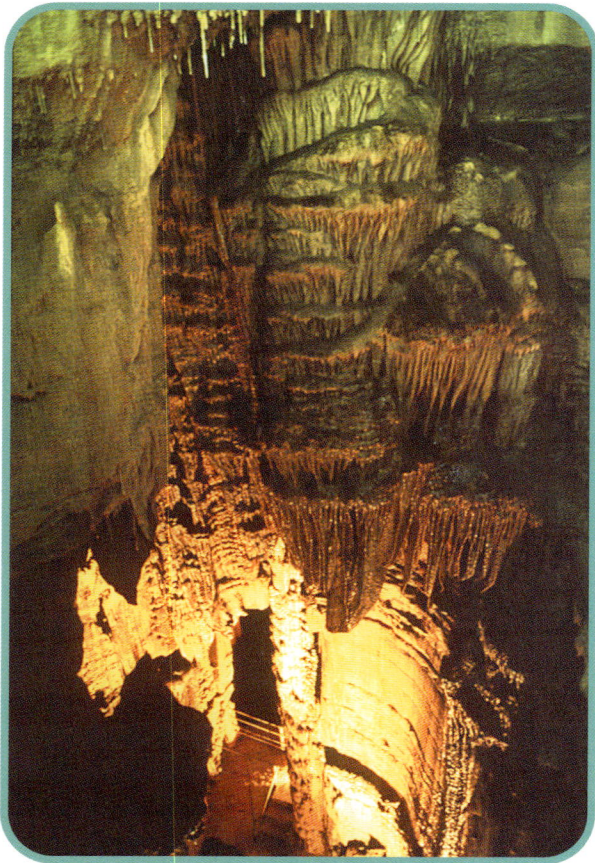

Mammoth Cave was made a national park in 1941.

Deep beneath Kentucky is the world's largest underground cave, known as Mammoth Cave. It includes more than 300 miles of known passages and even more that have not yet been explored. Visitors to Mammoth Cave National Park, which is located in central Kentucky near Bowling Green, may see unique cave formations, including the towering 192-foot-high Mammoth Dome and the 105-foot-deep Bottomless Pit. Some of the cave's passages are covered with sparkling white crystals and others are filled with colorful carved pillars. Underground rivers flow through the cave's deepest chambers.

More than 200 species of animals, from worms and eyeless fish to bats and cave crickets, live in these pitch black caves. Visitors can explore parts of the caves by taking tours of the underground passages.

Children Trog Tours

While visiting the Mammoth Cave National Park, children are invited to take a special tour designed especially for them. Parents are not allowed on this children-only trek. To explore the dark cave passages, hardhats and headlamps are required as children crawl around on their hands and knees, learning about the animals that live in the caves.

Map of Kentucky

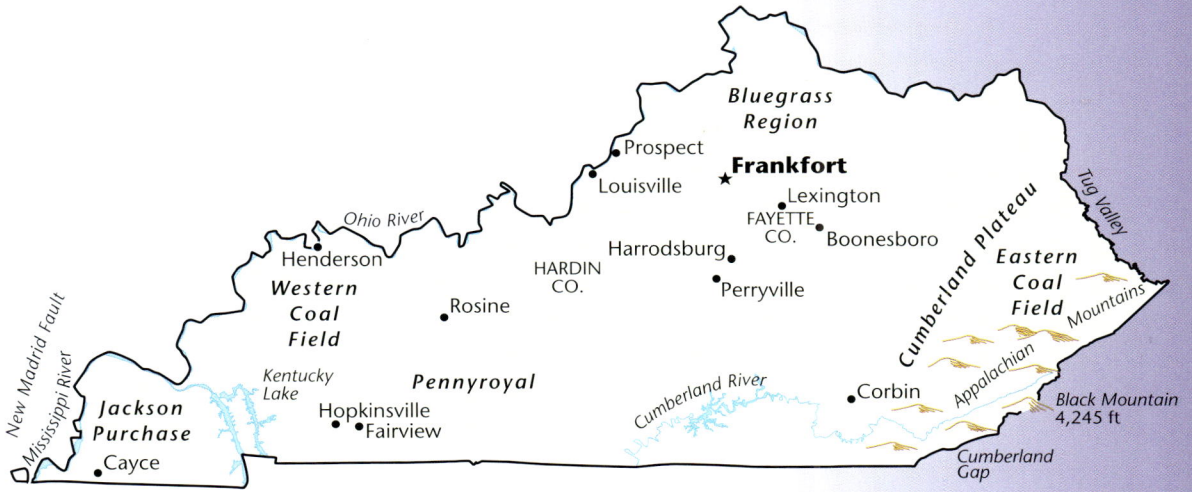

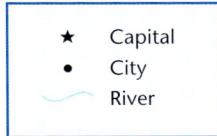

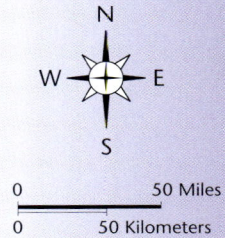

Bluegrass Region

Prospect

Frankfort ★

Louisville

Lexington

FAYETTE CO.

Boonesboro

Harrodsburg

Perryville

Cumberland Plateau

Tug Valley

Eastern Coal Field

Ohio River

Henderson

Western Coal Field

HARDIN CO.

Rosine

Mountains

Appalachian

New Madrid Fault

Mississippi River

Kentucky Lake

Pennyroyal

Cumberland River

Corbin

Black Mountain
4,245 ft

Jackson Purchase

Hopkinsville

Fairview

Cayce

Cumberland Gap

IND.

ILLINOIS

OHIO

Frankfort ★

W. VA.

MO.

KENTUCKY

VA.

ARK.

TENNESSEE

N.C.

S.C.

MISS.

ALABAMA

GEORGIA

★	Capital
•	City
～	River

N
W E
S

0 — 50 Miles

0 — 50 Kilometers

Glossary

abolitionists people who called for an end to slavery in the years before the Civil War (1861–1865)

assassinated to be killed

Bill of Rights part of a constitution that guarantees individual freedoms, such as freedom of speech and freedom of religion

Braille system of writing and printing used by people who are blind

caboose the last car on a freight train

capital offenses a serious crime that is punishable by death

cash crop a crop grown for direct sale and not for the feeding of livestock

civil cases those cases that relate to the rights of individuals

Civil War the war between the northern states, called the Union, and the southern states, known as the Confederacy, fought between 1861 and 1865

company store shops owned by a large employer who furnishes the chance to buy goods to their employees

Compromise of 1850 an act of the United States Congress that stated the new territories of New Mexico, Nevada, Arizona, and Utah would be left to decide for themselves whether to practice slavery or be admitted as free states.

Confederate States of America the name of the nation formed by the southern states of the U.S. in 1861, upon attempting to leave the Union

constitution a written document that outlines a plan of government

Cumberland Gap a natural passage through the Cumberland Plateau near the border of present-day Kentucky, Virginia, and Tennessee. Settlers heading west used the Cumberland Gap after Daniel Boone marked a trail though it in 1775.

federal government the national government of the United States, located in Washington, D.C.

felonies serious crimes, which are usually punishable by a penalty of more than one year in jail in addition to fines

feud a bitter fight between two people, families, or groups, often continuing for generations

flood plains flat, low-lying land near rivers or other bodies of water that frequently flood

ford a crossing

French and Indian War fought between 1754 and 1763, a conflict between the British and the French, along with their Native American allies. As a result of the war, the French were forced to give most of their land in North America to the British.

Islam a religion based on the acceptance of Muhammad as the last prophet of God and the Koran as the holy teachings of God

jurisdiction the power to interpret the law within a certain area

legend a popular story handed down from generation

legislature the branch of government that makes laws

misdemeanors less serious crimes

Missouri Compromise of 1820 an act of the United State Congress that admitted Maine as a free state and allowed no restrictions on slavery in the new state of Missouri, in an effort to maintain the balance of power between slave and free states

New Madrid Fault Line a crack in the earth's crust in Kentucky, Illinois, Tennessee, Arkansas, and Missouri near the Mississippi River.

patented something created or developed by someone that is protected by the United States Government

plateau a high area of land

precipitation rain or snow

reconstructed built again

reformers people who seek to change laws or social practices which they see as bad

Revolutionary War war that the Thirteen Colonies fought for independence from Great Britain from 1775 to 1783

rural having to do with the country, rather than the city

secession to withdraw formally from membership in an organization or union

states' rights the rights and powers of the state governments, especially those not granted the federal government by the U.S. Constitution

tax revenues the money government collects from taxes

Triple Crown horse racing title won by three-year-old horse that wins the Kentucky Derby, the Preakness, and the Belmont Stakes

Union of, or relating to those who remained loyal to the United States during the Civil War

World War I a war fought from 1914 to 1918, in which Great Britain, France, the United States, and their allies defeated Germany, Austria-Hungary, and their allies

World War II a war fought from 1939 to 1945, in which Great Britain, France, the Soviet Union, the United States, and their allies defeated Germany, Italy, and Japan

More Books to Read

Riehle, Mary Ann McCabe and Wes Burgiss. *B Is for Bluegrass: A Kentucky Alphabet.* Discover America State by State, Alphabet series. Chelsea, MN: Sleeping Bear Press, 2002.

Schott, Jane A. *Abraham Lincoln.* History Marker Bio series. Minneapolis, MN: Lerner Publishing, 2002.

Williams, Suzanne M. *Kentucky.* Danbury, CT: Children's Press, 1999.

Index

About the Authors

Maki and **Michelle Aki Becker** live in Brooklyn, New York. Maki is a journalist, and Michelle works in publishing.

D. J. Ross is a writer and educator with more than 25 years of experience in education. He has lived most of his life in the Midwest and still frequently visits Kentucky. He now lives in Ohio with his three basset hounds.